STAY UNDER THE SEA!

DIFFERENT ISN'T UGLY

OH, MY ACHING BACK!

THREE BOOK REVIEWS

by Cynthia Swain

Table of Contents

BOOK REVIEWS

What is a book review?

A book review is a composition that evaluates a book. In a book review, the reviewer, or critic, describes what happens in the book, and shares opinions about the book. The critic discusses what is good about the book, and what is bad about it. The critic uses details from the book to support his or her opinions.

What is the purpose of a book review?

Many people want to know about a book before they read it. They want to know what the book is about and if it is the "right" book for them. A book review helps readers decide whether to read a book

Who is the audience for a book review?

When an author writes a book, he or she has an audience in mind. The audience is all of the people interested in the subject. When a critic writes a book review, he or she has an audience in mind, too. The critic writes to all of the people who might want to read the book that he or she is reviewing.

How do you read a book review?

Pay attention to the plot, characters, and subject matter. Ask yourself, "Would this book interest me? Did it interest the reviewer? How can I tell?" Thin about how the reviewer rated the book. What did the critic like? What did he or she not like? Did he or she give good reasons for his or her opinions? After you read a review, ask yourself, "Do I want to read the book now?"

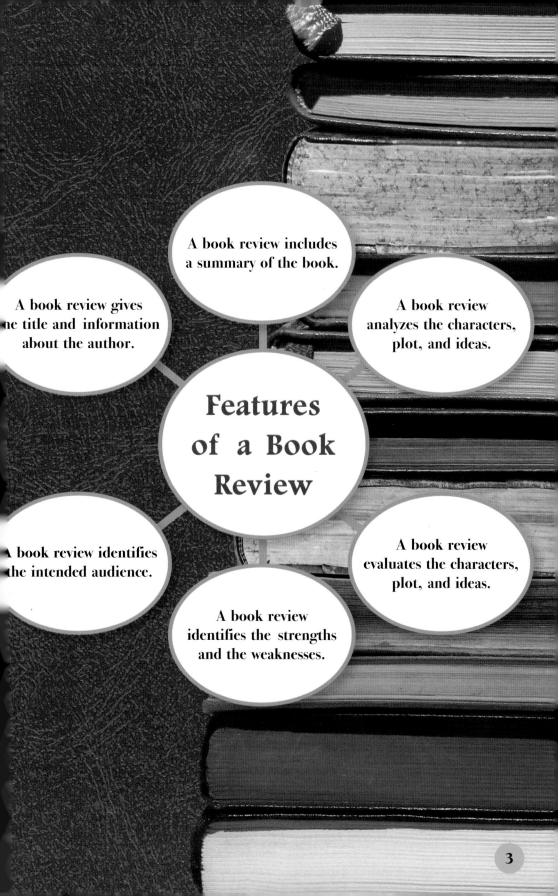

A book review includes a summary of the book.

A book review gives the title and information about the author.

A book review analyzes the characters, plot, and ideas.

Features of a Book Review

A book review identifies the intended audience.

A book review evaluates the characters, plot, and ideas.

A book review identifies the strengths and the weaknesses.

The Power of Reviews

Hans Christian Andersen was a famous writer. He was born in Odense, Denmark, in 1805. He died in Copenhagen in 1875 He wrote more than 150 fairy tales during his lifetime. Some of his tales had happy endings. Others were very sad. Andersen heard many of these tales when he was a child. His most famous tales are "The Little Mermaid," "The Ugly Duckling," and "The Princess and the Pea."

When Andersen's tales were first published, not everyone liked them. Book reviewers in Denmark thought that his writing was childish. People who read the book reviews didn't buy many of Andersen's books.

Andersen was angry and hurt. He said that the reviewers were being unfair. They didn't understand that his stories were meant for everyone. The stories were written for adults and children alike to appreciate.

In 1836, a reviewer from France visited Andersen in Denmark This reviewer liked Andersen's stories. He published a review that praised the stories. The review made readers want to buy Andersen's books.

Today, more than 150 years later, Andersen's fairy tales are still popular all over the world. There are even statues of him and the Ugly Duckling in Central Park in New York City.

▲ Statues of Hans Christian Andersen and the Ugly Duckling still sit in Central Park today.

Tools Writers Use
Strong Verbs

Which sounds better: "I talked loudly" or "I shouted"? Yes, **shouted** is a stronger verb, or action word. **Shouted** doesn't need an adverb, such as **loudly**, to make it better. We already know that **shouting** is loud. Another way to use strong verbs is to choose synonyms that specifically describe an action. These words help show, rather than tell, what happened. For example, do you **walk** to class, or do you **stride**, **amble**, **shuffle**, or **saunter**? Finally, authors use strong verbs to shorten, or tighten sentences. Example: "I **designed** the poster" (verb: **designed**) rather than "I **was** the designer of the poster" (verb: **was**).

Stay Under the Sea!

A young mermaid rises out of the sea for the first time. She falls in love with a handsome prince. She makes a deal with a devil of a sea witch. Will she get her prince? Hans Christian Andersen wrote "The Little Mermaid" in 1837. It is probably his most popular story. Perhaps you have read a version of the story. Maybe you have seen the movie. But watch out! The original story is different. It is beautiful, but very, very sad. If you like happily-ever-after endings, this story is not for you.

The story begins deep below the surface of the sea. Hidden there is the Sea King's castle. "Its walls are built of coral," Andersen writes. "The roof is formed of shells." The author's descriptions are so vivid that you will feel as though you are under the sea. In fact, Andersen is a master of description!

The Little Mermaid is the youngest daughter of the Sea King. She is beautiful and has a sweet voice. She has five sisters. At age fifteen, each sister may rise above the ocean to explore Earth. One by one, each sister takes her turn. They each bring back exciting stories of life on land. The author describes each sister's first visit in detail. Although I liked the descriptions, I admit that I got as impatient as the Little Mermaid. I wanted to read *her* story!

Finally, the Little Mermaid turns fifteen. She swims to the surface. It is evening. Through the vivid language, we envision what the Little Mermaid sees. "The clouds were tinted with crimson and gold, and through the glimmering twilight beamed the evening star in all its beauty," writes Andersen. "The sea was calm, and the air mild and fresh." The Little Mermaid spots a handsome prince on a ship. If only she hadn't!

A terrible storm erupts. The ship is wrecked. The prince is about to drown. The Little Mermaid drags him to the shore and leaves him on the rocks. He doesn't know that she has saved his life.

When he wakes up, he sees a different girl and falls in love with her. Things do not look good for the Little Mermaid—and they only get worse. I felt so sorry for her.

But the Little Mermaid is **innocent** and in love. She is **determined** to marry the prince. So she visits a witch. This witch agrees to give her a magic potion. The potion will turn the Little Mermaid's tail into legs. But there is a terrible price. The Little Mermaid must give her voice to the witch. In addition, her legs will cause her great pain. When the Little Mermaid walks, each step will feel like a dagger is stabbing her.

Only in a fairy tale would someone agree to this deal! I wanted the Little Mermaid to forget about the prince. I wanted her to say, "I don't need this prince to be happy! I can find someone else. I can be happy without any prince!" If Hans Christian Andersen had written this story today, maybe the Little Mermaid would say those things. Maybe the ending would be different.

Still, I liked the Little Mermaid. She was **gentle** and kind. Her actions (which I won't reveal) prove this. The prince was the sorry one. He could not see how **extraordinary** the Little Mermaid was. He didn't appreciate her.

There is much to admire in "The Little Mermaid." Andersen creates a rich world with his words. He makes you care deeply about the Little Mermaid. But don't expect her to win the prince's love. Her fate is sad. Have some tissues handy!

REREAD THE BOOK REVIEW

Understand the Review

- What story did the critic review? Who was the author of the story?
- What characters were in the story? What did the reviewer think of each character?
- What parts of the book did the critic think were weak? What parts were strong? How did she support her evaluations?

Analyze the Tools Writers Use

Strong Verbs

Reread the sentences with the following strong verbs. What images or pictures do you see as you reread these sentences?

- rise (page 7)
- swims (page 8)
- spots (page 8)
- drags (page 8)

Focus on Words

Adjectives That Describe Characters

In a review, writers use many words to describe the characters. In this review, for example, the writer uses the word **innocent** to describe the Little Mermaid. Make a chart like the one below. Find these other adjectives that also describe her. Then write a synonym for each word.

Page	Adjective	Synonym
8	innocent	
8	determined	
10	gentle	
10	extraordinary	

Different Isn't Ugly

A mother duck warms her eggs. Finally the eggs begin to crack—all but one egg, that is. So the mother duck sits and sits and sits. Finally the last duckling appears. But this duckling is different from his brothers and sisters. He is big. He looks **peculiar**. He doesn't walk the way ducks walk. Other ducks bite him. The chickens peck at him. His brothers and sisters tease him. Even his own mother wishes he had not been born. You cannot read this tale without feeling sorry for the Ugly Duckling.

Hans Christian Andersen published "The Ugly Duckling" in 1844. It is believed that the story was based on his own life. Growing up, he was very tall. He was not thought of as handsome. Children made fun of him. Maybe Andersen wanted to teach people a lesson. His story reminds us that everyone is special. It shows that you can be different from everyone else and still be beautiful.

The poor Ugly Duckling feels so **unwanted** that he runs away from home. Alone in the world, he meets many strangers—most of whom are mean. Then a flock of wild geese invite him to join them. Then hunters shoot many of the geese. The Ugly Duckling is left unharmed. He decides that he must be too **hideous** for the hunters to spend even a single shot on him.

Then the Ugly Duckling lives with an old woman. The woman's cat and hen tell the Ugly Duckling that he has no useful skills. The Ugly Duckling feels even worse about himself.

I wished that I could tell the Ugly Duckling not to listen to those creatures. Who were they to pass judgment on him? But he believes them. He can't help it. He has never been told by anyone that he has good qualities.

Finally, the Ugly Duckling finds a pond to swim in. The season changes from summer to autumn. Then winter comes. The Ugly Duckling almost freezes to death. Readers start to wonder if life will ever get better for the Ugly Duckling. Then one day, the Ugly Duckling looks up and spies something incredible. He sees several large birds. They have big wings and long necks. "How graceful they are," thinks the Ugly Duckling. He doesn't know what kind of birds they are. Still, he longs to be one of them.

You'll have to read the story to find out what happens next. And you should read the story. Everyone needs to read this tale. After all, most of us have felt like the Ugly Duckling sometime in our lives. This story helps us find the beauty in ourselves.

My only complaint is that the story ends too quickly. I wish that Andersen had written more. What would have happened had the Ugly Duckling gone back home? What would he have said to all of those animals that treated him badly? He could have taught them a lesson. But then great stories always leave us wanting more.

REREAD THE BOOK REVIEW

Understand the Review

- What story did the critic review? Who was the author of the story?
- Who were the characters? What did you learn about them?
- What did the critic like about this fairy tale? How do you know?
- Why does the critic think everyone should read this tale?

Analyze the Tools Writers Use

Strong Verbs

Reread the sentences with the following strong verbs. What images or pictures do you see as you reread these sentences?

- warms (page 13)
- peck (page 13)
- spies (page 14)
- longs (page 14)

Focus on Words

Adjectives That Describe Characters

Make a chart like the one below. Find these adjectives from the review that describe the Ugly Duckling. Can you provide a synonym for each word?

Page	Adjective	Synonym
13	peculiar	
13	unwanted	
13	hideous	

Oh, My Aching Back!

The reviewer tries to hook readers by telling them how this tale is different from other fairy tales.

There's a prince. There's a princess. There's a king, a queen, and a castle. But where are the dragons, witches, or evil spells?

"The Princess and the Pea" is not your typical fairy tale. This one breaks the rules. In fact, you could even say it's **goofy**. Hans Christian Andersen published the tale in 1835. He thought it would amuse people. Well, he was right about that! Everyone will enjoy this story.

The reviewer identifies the title and author of the tale.

The plot of "The Princess and the Pea" is downright **preposterous**. A prince has roamed the world looking for a "real" princess. "He traveled all over the world to find one," writes Andersen, "but nowhere could he get what he wanted." Andersen makes it sound as though princes go shopping for their princesses. He is obviously having fun with the fairy tale genre.

The reviewer summarizes the plot. She includes a quote from the story to help show that "The Princess and the Pea" is a funny fairy tale.

Apparently this prince doesn't have a very successful shopping spree. "There was always something about them that was not as it should be," explains Andersen. Readers must draw their own conclusions about why. Was the prince too picky? Did he not know what to look for?

The writer never really lets us get to know the prince. The story doesn't have a lot of character development. But that's part of the fun. All we know is that the prince comes home empty-handed and sad.

Then things really get interesting! One stormy night, there's a knock at the castle door. A young woman is standing outside in the pouring rain. She claims to be a princess. But she doesn't really look like a princess, says Andersen. What does a real princess look like? Again, readers must decide for themselves. I think that Andersen is making gentle fun of the princess stereotype.

In fairy tales, princesses usually arrive in big carriages. They have servants. They wear beautiful gowns. Their hair is perfect. But this princess is a mess! She's alone. She's on foot. And rain is dripping down her hair, clothes, and shoes. She is the anti-princess!

The old queen obviously doesn't believe that the young woman is truly a princess. She decides to put the woman to a test.

As you can guess from the story's title, the test involves a pea. It also involves many, many mattresses and the pea being placed underneath them. Even with the cushioning of all those mattresses, an authentic princess would be kept awake by the pea. Anyone else will not feel it, but the pea would bruise the skin of a princess.

Again, Andersen spoofs the princess stereotype. A real princess is delicate, he seems to tell us. She is more sensitive than other people.

Of course, the queen's test is **absurd** In a different story, the princess might say, "You expect me to sleep on twenty mattresses?" But in this story, she climbs right on without complaint. Will she fall asleep? Or will she feel the pea digging into her back? Read the story to find out. You won't be disappointed.

The reviewer doesn't give away the ending. She wants her audience members to have a reason to read the book for themselves.

REREAD THE BOOK REVIEW

Understand the Review
- What characters did the critic mention? What did you learn about them?
- What is the story's plot? What does the critic think about it? How do you know?
- Did the critic like the story? Why or why not?

Analyze the Tools Writers Use
Strong Verbs
Reread the sentences with the following strong verbs. What images or pictures do you see as you reread these sentences?
- roamed (page 17)
- claims (page 18)
- bruise (page 18)
- spoofs (page 20)

Focus on Words
Adjectives That Describe the Plot
The critic didn't describe the characters in detail, but she did describe the plot. Make a chart like the one below. Find these adjectives and give a synonym for each word.

Page	Adjective	Synonym
17	goofy	
17	preposterous	
20	absurd	

THE WRITER'S CRAFT

How does a critic write a

BOOK REVIEW?

Reread "Oh, My Aching Back!" and think about how the critic put the review together.

1. ## Choose a Book to Write About

In a review, the critic must identify the title, the author, and when the book was written. For example, this review was about the tale "The Princess and the Pea." It was written by Hans Christian Andersen in 1835.

2. ## Identify the Audience for the Book

Book reviewers should let readers know who might like the book, and who might not like it. What kind of reader would like the book? Is it for people with certain interests or knowledge? In this review, the critic says, "Everyone will enjoy this story."

3. Provide a Brief Summary

In a book review, the critic tells readers what the book is about. But the critic shouldn't give away every detail! Notice how this reviewer ends by saying, "Read the story to find out."

4. Identify and Give Examples of Strengths and Weaknesses

Book reviewers tell about the strengths and weaknesses in a book. They support their opinions with evidence from the book. Remember that book reviewers put their own voices into the reviews.

trengths	Supporting Evidence
reaks the fairy tale rules	The prince "shops" for a princess. The princess is a mess.
he story is fun	The queen puts the princess through a preposterous test.
eaknesses	**Supporting Evidence**
ry little character development	Readers don't get to know much about the prince.

Glossary

absurd   (ab-SERD) ridiculously unreasonable (page 20)

determined   (dih-TER-mend) not giving up; driven to succeed (page 8)

extraordinary   (ik-STROR-dih-nair-ee) exceptional (page 10)

gentle   (JEN-tul) kind; tender (page 10)

goofy   (GOO-fee) silly (page 17)

hideous   (HIH-dee-us) very unattractive; ugly (page 13)

innocent   (IH-nuh-sent) not guilty; blameless (page 8)

peculiar   (pih-KYOOL-yer) different from normal (page 13)

preposterous   (prih-PAHS-tuh-rus) lacking in wisdom or common sense (page 17)

unwanted   (un-WAN-ted) not needed (page 13)